I JOY

3 STEP

WRITING

2

I am books

Preview

1

Writing에 필요한 문법

해당 Unit의 영작을 위해 필요한 문법사항을
학습합니다.

2

Writing에 필요한 문법 확인

문제풀이를 통해 앞에서 배운 문법사항을
확인합니다.

3

Word List

해당 Unit의 영작을 위해 필요한
기본 단어를 익힙니다.

4

Step I: 문장 시작하기

영작할 문장의 주어 또는 주어와 서술부의
일부를 써보며 문장을 시작합니다.

5

Step 2: 문장 만들기

동사 또는 수식어를 활용하여 Step 1에서
시작한 문장을 이어나갑니다.

6

Step 3: 문장 완성하기

수식어 또는 수식어구를 활용하여 Step 2에서
만든 기본 문장들을 완성합니다.

7

Quiz Time

해당 Lesson에서 학습한 단어와 문법사항을
복습하고 영작활동을 통해 이를 적용합니다.

8

Check Up

다양한 유형의 활동을 통해 해당 Unit에서
학습한 것을 확인합니다.

영작을 위한 학생들의 이해도를
돕기 위해 간혹 어색한
한국말 표현이 있을 수 있음을
알려드립니다.

Contents

be동사 긍정문(과거)

Writing에 필요한 문법

① be동사 긍정문(과거)의 형태

be동사의 과거형: 주어에 따라 다르다.

주어	be동사의 과거형	
I	was	
You / We / They	were	hungry.
He / She / It	was	

② be동사 긍정문(과거) 맛보기

③ be동사 긍정문(과거)의 쓰임

예문	해석
My father was a farmer.	~였다
We were there together.	(~에) 있었다

* 부사 vs. 형용사

	부사	형용사
쓰임	형용사를 꾸며주는 단어로 형용사 앞에 위치	사람이나 사물의 상태나 성질이 어떠한지를 나타내는 단어
예시	very, really, so, too 등	yellow, small, beautiful, tall 등
예문	She was very pretty. 　　　부사　형용사	

Writing에 필요한 문법 확인

A. 다음 중 부사에 동그라미 하세요.

1 I was very small.

2 This book was too difficult.

3 The boy was really good.

4 The kids were so cute.

5 You were very brave.

B. 다음 중 알맞은 것을 고르세요.

1 Mom (was / were) happy.

2 We (was / were) baseball players.

3 The dog (was / were) hungry.

4 You (was / were) so kind.

5 The water (was / were) really cold.

C. 다음 문장을 과거형으로 바꾸세요.

1 My teacher is very good. _____

2 The cows are thirsty. _____

3 The house is very nice. _____

4 My friends are smart. _____

5 The sky is very blue. _____

D. 주어진 단어를 사용하여 문장을 완성하세요.

1 was / the box / heavy / .

_____

2 Dad / was / busy / very / .

_____

3 were / they / angry / .

_____

4 the birds / fast / were / .

_____

5 the test / difficult / was / .

_____

Word List

English	Korean	English	Korean
after work	퇴근 후	late	늦은
angry	화난	ready	준비된
excited	신이 난	thirsty	목이 마른
here	여기에	tired	피곤한
interesting	재미있는, 흥미로운	yesterday	어제

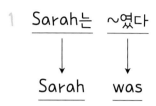 다음의 우리말 표현을 영어로 쓰세요.

1 Sarah는   ~였다

   ↓   ↓

  Sarah   was

2 나는   ~였다

_____

3 그 책은 (the book)   (~에) 있었다

_____

4 그 고양이들은 (the cats)   ~였다

_____

5 그 꽃들은 (the flowers)   ~였다

_____

6 엄마는 (Mom)   ~였다

_____

7 그 영화는 (the movie)   ~였다

_____

8 Rob은   ~였다

_____

9 그 학생들은 (the students)   ~였다

_____

10 우리는   ~였다

_____

 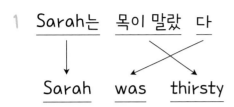 다음의 우리말 표현을 영어로 쓰세요.

1 <u>Sarah는</u> 목이 말랐 다

    <u>Sarah</u>   <u>was</u>   <u>thirsty</u>

2 나는 화났 다

_____

3 그 책은 여기에 있었다

_____

4 그 고양이들은 빨랐 다 (fast)

_____

5 그 꽃들은 아름다웠 다

_____

6 엄마는 피곤했 다

_____

7 그 영화는 재미있었 다

_____

8 Rob은 늦었 다

_____

9 그 학생들은 준비되었 다

_____

10 우리는 신이났 다

_____

Step 3 다음의 우리말 표현을 영어로 쓰세요.

1 Sarah는 매우 목이 말랐다.

   Sarah was very thirsty.

2 나는 너에게 (at you) 화났다.

   _____

3 그 책은 어제 여기에 있었다.

   _____

4 그 고양이들은 정말로 (really) 빨랐다.

   _____

5 그 꽃들은 대단히 (so) 아름다웠다.

   _____

6 엄마는 퇴근 후 피곤했다.

   _____

7 그 영화는 매우 (very) 재미있었다.

   _____

8 Rob은 학교에 (for school) 늦었다.

   _____

9 그 학생들은 그 시험을 치를 (for the test) 준비가 되었다.

   _____

10 우리는 그 여행에 대해 (about the trip) 신이 났다.

   _____

A. 빈칸을 채우세요.

English	Korean	English	Korean
after work			늦은
	화난		준비된
excited		thirsty	
	여기에		피곤한
interesting		yesterday	

B. 빈칸을 채우세요.

1 형용사를 꾸며주는 단어를 ＿＿＿＿＿＿＿ 라고 한다.

2 형용사는 사람이나 ＿＿＿＿＿＿＿ 의 상태나 성질이 어떠한지를
   나타내는 단어이다.

C. 다음 중 형용사와 부사에 동그라미 하세요.

1 She was very beautiful.

2 The girl was so happy.

3 The box was really heavy.

D. 그림을 보고 be동사와 주어진 단어를 사용하여 과거형 문장을 완성하세요.

1

2

3

4

Word Box

nice	baseball players	small	brave

1 John and Ken _____.

2 Gina _____.

3 The house _____ _____.

4 The firefighters _____.

Lesson 2

be동사 부정문(과거)

Writing에 필요한 문법

① be동사 부정문(과거)의 형태

be동사의 부정형: be동사 뒤에 not을 붙인다.

주어	be동사의 부정형(과거)	
I	was not(wasn't)	
You / They / We	were not(weren't)	busy.
He / She / It	was(wasn't)	

② be동사 부정문(과거) 맛보기

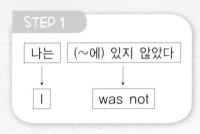

STEP 1

나는	(~에) 있지 않았다
↓	↓
I	was not

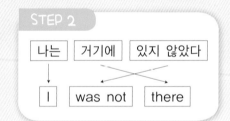

STEP 2

나는	거기에	있지 않았다
I	was not	there

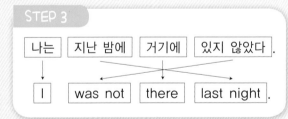

STEP 3

나는	지난 밤에	거기에	있지 않았다 .
I	was not	there	last night .

③ be동사 부정문(과거)의 쓰임

예문	해석
Jenny was not happy.	~하지 않았다
Tom wasn't a basketball player.	~가 아니었다
The kids were not there anymore.	(~에) 있지 않았다

단어	excited	exciting	interested	interesting
쓰임	누군가가 신이 난 상황을 표현할 때	무엇인가가 재미 있고 신난다는 것을 표현할 때	누군가가 무엇에 관심이 있다는 것을 표현할 때	무엇인가가 신기 하고 흥미롭다는 것을 표현할 때
예문	I was so excited!	The Viking ship was very exciting!	I was very interested in the book.	The book was very interesting!

Writing에 필요한 문법 확인

A. 다음 중 알맞은 것을 고르세요.

1　I (was not / were not) thirsty.

2　The movie (was not / were not) funny.

3　We (was not / were not) happy about the trip.

4　My boy (wasn't / weren't) excited about the concert.

5　Your pencils (wasn't / weren't) on the desk.

B. 다음 중 알맞은 것을 고르세요.

1　They were (interested / interesting) in the movie.

2　The show was (excited / exciting).

3　I was (tired / tiring) after the exercise.

4　The museum was very (interested / interesting).

5　My dog was (excited / exciting) about the snack.

C. 괄호 안의 단어가 들어갈 위치에 V 하세요.

1 The flowers were beautiful. (not)

2 The sky was clear. (not)

3 The small bug was cute. (not)

4 Dad was hungry. (not)

5 The box was big. (not)

D. be동사와 not을 사용하여 과거형 문장을 완성하세요.

1 I _____ a baseball player.

2 Jenny _____ kind to me.

3 The boys _____ tall.

4 The game _____ funny.

5 We _____ ready for the test.

Word List

English	Korean	English	Korean
delicious	맛있는	interesting	흥미로운
exam	시험	light	가벼운
excited	신이 난	puppy	강아지
here	여기에	tired	피곤한
hot	뜨거운	toy	장난감

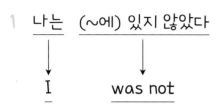 다음의 우리말 표현을 영어로 쓰세요.

1 <u>나는</u> <u>(~에) 있지 않았다</u>

   ↓   ↓

   <u>I</u>   <u>was not</u>

2 그 학생들은 (the students) ~하지 않았다

_____

3 그 책은 (the book) ~하지 않았다

_____

4 내 강아지는 (my puppy) ~하지 않았다

_____

5 Judy는 ~가 아니었다

_____

6 우리는 ~하지 않았다

_____

7 그 음식은 (the food) ~하지 않았다

_____

8 내 장난감은 (my toys) (~에) 있지 않았다

_____

9 그 커피는 (the coffee) ~하지 않았다

_____

10 내 부츠는 (my boots) ~하지 않았다

_____

 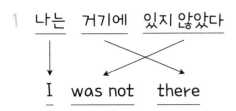 다음의 우리말 표현을 영어로 쓰세요.

1 나는 거기에 있지 않았다

    I was not there

2 그 학생들은 기분이 좋지 (happy) 않았다

_____

3 그 책은 흥미롭지 (interesting) 않았다

_____

4 내 강아지는 피곤해 하지 않았다

_____

5 Judy는 농구 선수가 (a baseball player) 아니었다

_____

6 우리는 신이 나지 않았다

_____

7 그 음식은 맛있지 않았다

_____

8 내 장난감은 여기에 있지 않았다

_____

9 그 커피는 뜨겁지 않았다

_____

10 내 부츠는 가볍지 않았다

_____

Step 3 다음의 우리말 표현을 영어로 쓰세요.

1 나는 지난 밤에 거기에 있지 않았다.

I was not there last night .

2 그 학생들은 그 시험에 대해 (about the exam) 기분이 좋지 않았다.

_____

3 그 책은 아주 (very) 흥미롭지는 않았다.

_____

4 내 강아지는 놀이 후에 (after the play) 피곤해하지 않았다.

_____

5 Judy는 고등학교에서 (in high school) 농구 선수가 아니었다.

_____

6 우리는 그 게임에 (about the game) 신이 나지 않았다.

_____

7 그 식당의 (at the restaurant) 음식은 맛있지 않았다.

_____

8 내 장난감은 어제 (yesterday) 여기에 있지 않았다.

_____

9 그 커피는 아주 (very) 뜨겁지는 않았다.

_____

10 내 부츠는 빗속에서 (in the rain) 가볍지 않았다.

_____

A. 빈칸을 채우세요.

English	Korean	English	Korean
delicious			흥미로운
exam		light	
	신이 난		강아지
here			피곤한
	뜨거운	toy	

B. 다음 중 알맞은 것을 고르세요.

1 I was so (excited / exciting) about the Viking ship!

2 She was (interested / interesting) in the book.

3 The books were very (interested / interesting)!

4 The Viking ship was (excited / exciting).

20

C. 그림을 보고 be동사와 not, 그리고 주어진 단어를 사용하여 과거형 문장을 완성하세요.

1

2

3

4

Word Box

fun	hungry	big	clear

1 The boy _____.

2 The box _____.

3 The sky _____.

4 The game _____.

Unit 1
Lesson 3

be동사 의문문(과거)

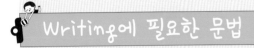

① be동사 의문문(과거)의 형태

be동사의 과거형	주어	
Was	I	
Were	you / they / we	busy?
Was	he / she / it	

② be동사 의문문(과거) 맛보기

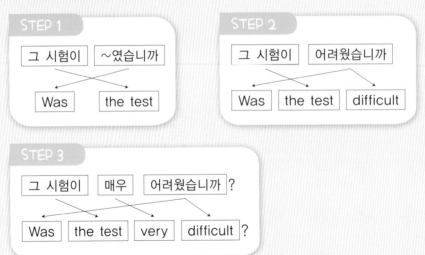

③ be동사 의문문(과거)의 쓰임

예문	해석
Q: Was the T-shirt big? A: Yes, it was. / No, it wasn't.	~였습니까?
Q: Were you at home yesterday? A: Yes, I was. / No, I wasn't.	(~에) 있었습니까?

＊ 동물을 대신하는 인칭대명사

– 북미권에서는 한 동물의 성별을 아는 경우에는 성별에 따라 인칭대명사 he, she 를 사용한다. 다만 동물의 성별을 모르고 수가 하나일 때는 대명사 it을 사용한다.

(예문) Was your cat sick? Yes, she was. / No, she wasn't.

My puppy was very small. But now he is a big boy.

Look at the little rabbit! It is so cute.

Writing에 필요한 문법 확인

A. be동사 의문문에 동그라미 하세요.

1　Was the bird cute?

2　Do you have homework?

3　Were you okay?

4　Do they play soccer after school?

5　Was Sarah sick yesterday?

B. 다음 중 알맞은 것을 고르세요.

1　(Was / Were) he nice to you?

2　(Was / Were) the flowers beautiful?

3　(Was / Were) the school big?

4　(Was / Were) your parents angry?

5　(Was / Were) Gina sleepy?

C. 대답을 완성하세요.

1 Was Tony hungry?   Yes, _____

2 Was your sister thirsty?   Yes, _____

3 Were they excited about the show? No, _____

4 Was the skirt small?   Yes, _____

5 Were you (당신들) there yesterday? No, _____

D. 다음 문장을 의문문으로 바꿔 쓰세요.

1 The food was delicious.

_____

2 They were happy.

_____

3 The car was expensive.

_____

4 Rob was tired.

_____

5 The movie was interesting.

_____

Word List

English	Korean	English	Korean
at home	집에	healthy	건강한
clean	깨끗한	late	늦은
difficult	어려운	sick	아픈
dirty	더러운	slow	느린
expensive	비싼	tree	나무

Step 1 다음의 우리말 표현을 영어로 쓰세요.

1 <u>그 시험은</u> <u>~였습니까</u>

<u>Was</u>   <u>the test</u>

2 그들은   ~였습니까

_____

3 그 접시는 (the plate)   ~였습니까

_____

4 그의 방은 (his room)   ~였습니까

_____

5 그 나무들은 (the trees)   ~였습니까

_____

6 그녀의 엄마는 (her mom)   ~였습니까

_____

7 그 콘서트는 (the concert)   ~였습니까

_____

8 그 바지는 (the pants)   ~였습니까

_____

9 당신의 컴퓨터는 (your computer)   ~였습니까

_____

10 당신은   (~에) 있었습니까

_____

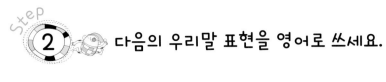

Step ② 다음의 우리말 표현을 영어로 쓰세요.

1 그 시험은 어려웠습니까

      Was the test difficult

2 그들은 늦었 습니까

_____

3 그 접시는 깨끗했 습니까

_____

4 그의 방은 더러웠 습니까

_____

5 그 나무들은 건강했 습니까

_____

6 그녀의 엄마는 아팠 습니까

_____

7 그 콘서트는 흥미진진했 습니까 (exciting)

_____

8 그 바지는 비쌌 습니까

_____

9 당신의 컴퓨터는 느렸 습니까

_____

10 당신은 집에 있었습니까

_____

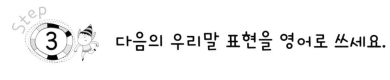

다음의 우리말 표현을 영어로 쓰세요.

1 그 시험이 **매우** 어려웠습니까?

Was the test **very** difficult?

2 그들은 **학교에** (for school) 늦었습니까?

_____

3 **그 탁자 위에** (on the table) 접시는 깨끗했습니까?

_____

4 그의 방은 **꽤** (quite) 더러웠습니까?

_____

5 그 나무들 **과 꽃들은** (and flowers) 건강했습니까?

_____

6 그녀의 엄마는 **매우** (very) 아팠습니까?

_____

7 그 콘서트는 흥미진진하 **고 재미있었** 습니까? (and fun)

_____

8 그 **파란** (blue) 바지는 비쌌습니까?

_____

9 **오늘 아침에** (this morning) 당신의 컴퓨터는 느렸습니까?

_____

10 **지난 밤에** (last night) 당신은 집에 있었습니까?

_____

A. 빈칸을 채우세요.

English	Korean	English	Korean
at home		healthy	
	깨끗한		늦은
	어려운	sick	
dirty			느린
	비싼	tree	

B. 빈칸을 채우세요.

북미권에서는 한 동물의 성별을 아는 경우에는 성별에 따라 _____,

she를 사용한다. 다만 동물의 성별을 모르고 수가 하나일 때는 대명사

_____ 을 사용한다.

C. 대명사를 사용하여 빈칸을 채우세요.

1 Was your cat sick? No, _____ wasn't.
   (당신의 고양이가 암컷인 경우)

2 My puppy was very small. But now _____ is a big boy.
   (내 강아지가 수컷인 경우)

3 Look at the little rabbit! _____ is so cute.
   (토끼의 성별을 모르는 경우)

D. 그림을 보고 be동사와 주어진 단어를 사용하여 과거형 문장을 완성하세요.

1

2 Sarah

3 Gina   Jason

4 Tom   Jenny

Word Box

sick   late   angry   interesting

1 _____ the animated movie _____?

2 _____ Sarah _____?

3 _____ Gina and Jason _____?

4 _____ Tom and Jenny _____ for school?

A. 주어진 단어를 사용하여 문장을 완성하세요.

was	were

1 _____ you at home?

2 _____ Tony hungry?

3 _____ the green pants expensive?

4 _____ her room dirty?

5 _____ they okay?

B. 다음 문장에서 be동사를 찾아 동그라미 하세요.

1 We were thirsty.

2 The water was cold.

3 The sky was very blue.

4 Dad was busy.

5 They were baseball players.

C. 주어진 단어를 사용하여 문장을 완성하세요.

1 nice / was / the house / .

_____

2 weren't / the boxes / heavy / .

_____

3 the museum / big / was / .

_____

4 were / healthy / the plants / ?

_____

D. 다음 문장을 영작하세요.

1 그 시험은 매우 어려웠다. (very difficult)

_____

2 당신은 나에게 화나 있었습니까? (at me)

_____

3 우리는 그 여행에 대해 신이 났다. (about the trip)

_____

4 그 커피는 뜨겁지 않았다. (hot)

_____

일반동사 긍정문(과거)

Writing에 필요한 문법

① 일반동사 긍정문(과거)의 형태

일반동사의 과거형: 주어에 상관없이 같은 형태를 가진다.

주어	일반동사의 과거형	
I		
You / They / We	ate	a lot.
He / She / It		

② 일반동사 긍정문(과거) 맛보기

STEP 1

우리는	공부했다
↓	↓
We	studied

STEP 2

우리는	과학을	공부했다
We	studied	science

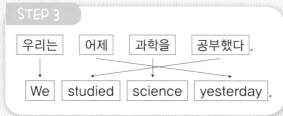

STEP 3

우리는	어제	과학을	공부했다 .
We	studied	science	yesterday .

③ 일반동사 긍정문(과거)의 쓰임

쓰임	예문	해석
이미 지나간 일을 표현할 때	I watched a movie last week.	~했(었)다
	She went to the museum yesterday.	

＊ 일반동사의 과거형 만드는 규칙

동사	규칙	예시
대부분의 동사	동사원형에 ed를 붙인다.	walk – walked push – pushed
-e로 끝나는 동사	동사원형에 d를 붙인다.	love – loved dance – danced
자음＋y로 끝나는 동사	y를 i로 고치고 ed를 붙인다.	cry – cried study – studied
모음 한 개＋자음 한 개로 끝나는 동사	마지막 자음을 하나 더 붙이고 ed를 붙인다.	drop – dropped plan – planned

＊ 불규칙하게 변하는 동사의 과거형

(예시)

현재형	run	come	read	think	eat	see	go
과거형	ran	came	read	thought	ate	saw	went

Writing에 필요한 문법 확인

A. 다음 중 알맞은 것을 고르세요.

1 He (walked / walkked) to school.

2 I (droped / dropped) the ball.

3 Henry and John (played / plaied) soccer.

4 We (goed / went) to Kelly's house.

5 William (readed / read) the book.

B. 주어진 동사의 과거형을 쓰세요.

현재형	과거형	현재형	과거형
run		eat	
come		see	

C. 주어진 동사를 이용하여 과거형 문장을 완성하세요.

1 They _____ dinner together. (eat)

2 Sarah _____ running. (stop)

3 We _____ a computer game. (play)

4 I _____ him very much. (like)

5 The baby _____ all day. (cry)

D. 다음 문장을 과거형 문장으로 바꿔 쓰세요.

1 Peter read a comic book.

   _____

2 I listen to music.

   _____

3 They stay at home.

   _____

4 Nancy talks on the phone.   .

   _____

5 He goes to bed at 9 o'clock.

   _____

Word List

English	Korean	English	Korean
dance/danced	춤을 추다	open/opened	열다
eat/ate	먹다	read/read	읽다
give/gave	주다	show/showed	보여주다
go/went	가다	study/studied	공부하다
love/loved	사랑하다	work/worked	일하다

 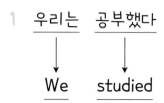 다음의 우리말 표현을 영어로 쓰세요.

1 우리는   공부했다
    ↓   ↓
   We   studied

2 Kelly는   보여주었다

   _____

3 그는   사랑했다

   _____

4 그 여자는 (the woman)   읽었다

   _____

5 나는   갔다

   _____

6 그녀는   일했다

   _____

7 그들은   춤을 추었다

   _____

8 Mr. Kim은   열었다

   _____

9 그 소녀는 (the girl)   먹었다

   _____

10 나는   주었다

   _____

 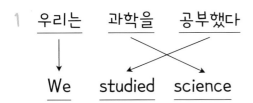 다음의 우리말 표현을 영어로 쓰세요.

1 우리는   과학을   공부했다

We   studied   science

2 Kelly는   사진을 (a picture) 보여주었다

_____

3 그는   그의 고양이를 (his cat) 사랑했다

_____

4 그 여자는   신문을 (a newspaper) 읽었다

_____

5 나는   교회에 (to church) 갔다

_____

6 그녀는   그 회사에서 (at the company) 일했다

_____

7 그들은   함께 (together) 춤을 추었다

_____

8 Mr. Kim은   음식점을 (a restaurant) 열었다

_____

9 그 소녀는   햄버거를 (a hamburger) 먹었다

_____

10 나는   선물을 (a gift) 주었다

_____

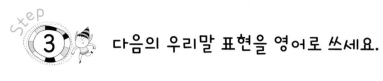

3 다음의 우리말 표현을 영어로 쓰세요.

1 우리는 어제 과학을 공부했다.

We studied science yesterday .

2 Kelly는 나에게 (to me) 사진을 보여주었다.

_____

3 그는 그의 고양이를 매우 많이 (very much) 사랑했다.

_____

4 그 여자는 아침에 (in the morning) 신문을 읽었다.

_____

5 나는 지난 일요일에 (last Sunday) 교회에 갔다.

_____

6 그녀는 작년에 (last year) 그 회사에서 일했다.

_____

7 그들은 그 파티에서 (at the party) 함께 춤을 추었다.

_____

8 Mr. Kim은 지난 주에 (last week) 그 음식점을 열었다.

_____

9 그 소녀는 점심으로 (for lunch) 햄버거를 먹었다.

_____

10 나는 내 친구에게 (to my friend) 선물을 주었다.

_____

A. 빈칸을 채우세요.

English	Korean	English	Korean
	춤을 추다	open/opened	
eat/ate			읽다
give/gave		show/showed	
go/went		study/studied	
	사랑하다		일하다

B. 빈칸을 채우세요.

＊일반동사의 과거형 만드는 규칙

1 대부분의 동사는 동사원형에 　　　　　　를 붙인다.

2 -e로 끝나는 동사는 동사원형에 　　　　　　를 붙인다.

3 자음 + y로 끝나는 동사는 y를 　　　　　　로 고치고 　　　　　　를 붙인다.

4 모음 한 개 + 자음 한 개로 끝나는 동사는 　　　　　　을 하나 더 붙이고 ed를 붙인다.

C. 그림을 보고 주어진 동사를 이용하여 과거형 문장을 완성하세요.

1

2

3

4

Sally

Word Box

| move | drop | read | watch |

1 My dad _____ a book last Sunday.

2 They _____ a table yesterday.

3 The woman _____ an egg.

4 Sally _____ TV last night.

일반동사 부정문(과거)

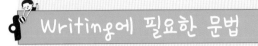
Writing에 필요한 문법

① 일반동사 부정문(과거)의 형태

주어	did not	동사원형
I		
You / We / They	did not(didn't)	move.
He / She / It		

② 일반동사 부정문(과거) 맛보기

STEP 1

그는	~하지 않았다
↓	↓
He	didn't

STEP 2

그는	고치지 않았다
↓	
He	didn't fix

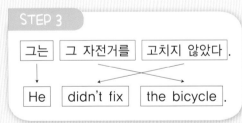

STEP 3

그는	그 자전거를	고치지 않았다
↓		
He	didn't fix	the bicycle

③ 일반동사 부정문(과거)의 쓰임

예문	해석
My aunt didn't teach science.	~하지 않았(었)다
We didn't clean the house.	

* a/an

- '한 개, 한 명, 또는 하나의'라는 의미로 명사 앞에 a 또는 an을 붙인다.
- 대부분의 명사 앞에 a를 붙이지만, 첫 소리가 a, e, i, o, u로 소리나는 명사 앞에는 an을 붙인다.

  (예시) a book, a desk, a dog 등

  ㅤㅤㅤ an orange, an egg, an elephant 등

- a와 an은 명사 한 개를 나타낼 때에만 사용하므로, 명사가 두 개 이상일 때에는 사용할 수 없다.

  (예시) a pencil ㅤ Ⅹ two pencils ㅤ an apple ㅤ Ⅹ five apples

Writing에 필요한 문법 확인

A. <보기>의 단어들을 해당되는 곳에 쓰세요.

> <보기> girl ant cat car umbrella egg teacher octopus

1 a _____

2 an _____

B. 다음 중 틀린 부분을 고쳐 바르게 쓰세요. 틀린 부분이 없다면 Ⅹ 하세요.

1 I didn't eat a apple.

_____

2 They didn't see an dog.

_____

3 Max and Julie didn't buy an egg.

_____

4 She didn't make a sandwich.

_____

5 He didn't give me a ice cream.

_____

C. 다음 중 알맞은 것을 고르세요.

1 I (wasn't / didn't) make a cake.

2 They (don't / didn't) play soccer yesterday.

3 Mike didn't (go / goes) to school.

4 She didn't (meet / met) her friends.

5 We (don't / didn't) buy a car last week.

D. 다음 문장을 부정문으로 바꿔 쓰세요.

1 Sunny liked milk.

_____

2 I invited my friends.

_____

3 He lived in Busan.

_____

4 Karen ate bread for breakfast.

_____

5 We walked to the bus stop.

_____

Word List

English	Korean	English	Korean
brush/brushed	닦다	fix/fixed	고치다
buy/bought	사다	go shopping/ went shopping	쇼핑하러 가다
close/closed	닫다	know/knew	알다
drink/drank	마시다	meet/met	만나다
drive/drove	운전하다	smile/smiled	미소 짓다

 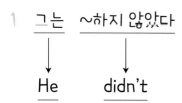 다음의 우리말 표현을 영어로 쓰세요.

1 그는 ~하지 않았다
   ↓   ↓
   He   didn't

2 나는   ~하지 않았다

_____

3 Serena는   ~하지 않았다

_____

4 내 삼촌은 (my uncle) ~하지 않았다

_____

5 그녀는   ~하지 않았다

_____

6 Jay는   ~하지 않았다

_____

7 엄마는   ~하지 않았다

_____

8 그 소년은 (the boy) ~하지 않았다

_____

9 당신은   ~하지 않았다

_____

10 그 여자는 (the woman) ~하지 않았다

_____

다음의 우리말 표현을 영어로 쓰세요.

1 <u>그는</u>   <u>고치지 않았다</u>

    ↓   ↓

  <u>He</u>   <u>didn't fix</u>

2 나는   마시지   않았다

_____

3 Serena는   만나지   않았다

_____

4 내 삼촌은   운전하지   않았다

_____

5 그녀는   쇼핑하러 가지   않았다

_____

6 Jay는   닦지   않았다

_____

7 엄마는   사지   않았다

_____

8 그 소년은   미소 짓지   않았다

_____

9 당신은   닫지   않았다

_____

10 그 여자는   알지   않았다

_____

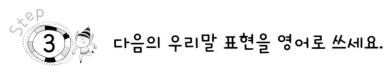

3 다음의 우리말 표현을 영어로 쓰세요.

1 그는 그 자전거를 고치지 않았디.

He didn't fix the bicycle .

2 나는 커피를 (coffee) 마시지 않았다.

_____

3 Serena는 그녀의 선생님을 (her teacher) 만나지 않았다.

_____

4 내 삼촌은 그 트럭을 (the truck) 운전하지 않았다.

_____

5 그녀는 어제 (yesterday) 쇼핑하러 가지 않았다.

_____

6 Jay는 그의 이를 (his teeth) 닦지 않았다.

_____

7 엄마는 채소들을 (vegetables) 사지 않았다.

_____

8 그 소년은 나에게 (at me) 미소 짓지 않았다.

_____

9 당신은 그 창문을 (the window) 닫지 않았다.

_____

10 그 여자는 그 사실에 대해 (about the fact) 알지 않았다.

_____

A. 빈칸을 채우세요.

English	Korean	English	Korean
	닦다	fix/fixed	
buy/bought			쇼핑하러 가다
	닫다		알다
drink/drank		meet/met	
drive/drove			미소 짓다

B. 빈칸을 채우세요.

1 '한 개, 한 명, 또는 하나의'라는 의미로 명사 앞에 [ ]   또는
[ ]   을 붙인다.

2 대부분의 명사 앞에 a를 붙이지만, 첫 소리가 [ ]   로 소리
나는 명사 앞에는 an을 붙인다.

3 a와 an은 명사 한 개를 나타낼 때에만 사용하므로, 명사가 [ ]
이상일 때에는 사용할 수 없다.

C. 다음 중 알맞은 것을 고르세요.

1 I saw (a / an) tiger at the zoo.

2 She bought (a / an) umbrella.

3 He ate (a / an) apple in the morning.

4 They carried (a / an) desk.

D. 그림을 보고 주어진 동사를 이용하여 과거형 문장을 완성하세요.

1

2

3

4

Word Box

| listen | visit | eat | write |

1 The boy _____ a letter.

2 The girl _____ to music.

3 I _____ my grandparents yesterday.

4 Jessica _____ the cookies.

일반동사 의문문(과거)

Writing에 필요한 문법

① 일반동사 의문문(과거)의 형태

Did	주어	동사원형	
Did	I	walk	fast?
	you / they / we		
	he / she / it		

② 일반동사 의문문(과거) 맛보기

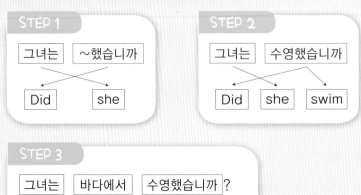

STEP 1
그녀는 ~했습니까
Did she

STEP 2
그녀는 수영했습니까
Did she swim

STEP 3
그녀는 바다에서 수영했습니까?
Did she swim in the sea?

③ 일반동사 의문문(과거)의 쓰임

예문	해석
Did you do your homework?	~했(었)습니까?
Did Mark stay at home?	

* 일반동사 의문문 (과거)에 대한 대답

– 긍정일 때는 'Yes, 주어 + did.'로 대답한다.

– 부정일 때는 'No, 주어 + didn't.'로 대답한다.

– 대답할 때의 주어는 알맞은 대명사를 사용한다.

(예문) Q: Did Sally read a book? A: Yes, she did. / No, she didn't.

Q: Did you teach English? A: Yes, I did. / No, I didn't.

Writing에 필요한 문법 확인

A. 알맞은 대답에 동그라미 하세요.

1 Q: Did Jason paint a picture?
   A: (Yes, he did. / No, she didn't.)

2 Q: Did she enjoy the party?
   A: (Yes, she did. / Yes, she didn't.)

3 Q: Did you go shopping yesterday?
   A: (No, I did. / No, I didn't.)

4 Q: Did they play baseball?
   A: (Yes, they did. / No, we didn't.)

5 Q: Did you and Tom walk to school?
   A: (Yes, you did. / No, we didn't.)

B. 다음 질문에 대한 대답을 완성하세요.

1 Q: Did the boy and girl study together? A: _____ , they didn't.

2 Q: Did you cook dinner?   A: _____ , I did.

3 Q: Did Sam meet his friends?   A: No, _____ .

4 Q: Did it rain yesterday?   A: Yes, _____ .

5 Q: Did Julie buy the flowers?   A: No, _____ .

C. 주어진 단어를 사용하여 문장을 완성하세요.

1 did / milk / you / drink / ? _____

2 he / English / did / study / ? _____

3 help / the man / her / did / ? _____

4 Jay / did / dinner / have / ? _____

5 did / yesterday / she / cry / ? _____

D. 다음 문장을 의문문으로 바꿔 쓰세요.

1 The family had a puppy.

_____

2 You bought a jacket.

_____

3 Kelly knew about him.

_____

4 They went to the zoo.

_____

5 He lived in Seoul.

_____

Word List

English	Korean	English	Korean
call/called	전화하다	make/made	만들다
come/came	오다	plant/planted	심다
cook/cooked	요리하다	stay/stayed	머물다
find/found	찾다	swim/swam	수영하다
go skiing/ went skiing	스키를 타러 가다	write/wrote	쓰다

 다음의 우리말 표현을 영어로 쓰세요.

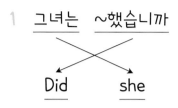

1 그녀는 ~했습니까

    Did   she

2 Mike는 ~했습니까

_____

3 당신은 ~했습니까

_____

4 Billy는 ~했습니까

_____

5 그들은 ~했습니까

_____

6 Mary는 ~했습니까

_____

7 그는 ~했습니까

_____

8 당신의 엄마와 아빠는 ~했습니까

_____

9 그녀는 ~했습니까

_____

10 그는 ~했습니까

_____

 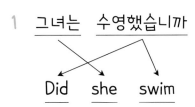 다음의 우리말 표현을 영어로 쓰세요.

1 <u>그녀는</u> <u>수영했습니까</u>

<u>Did</u> <u>she</u> <u>swim</u>

2 Mike는 썼 습니까

_____

3 당신은 요리했 습니까

_____

4 Billy는 찾았 습니까

_____

5 그들은 스키를 타러 갔 습니까

_____

6 Mary는 전화했 습니까

_____

7 그는 심었 습니까

_____

8 당신의 엄마와 아빠는 머물렀 습니까

_____

9 그녀는 만들었 습니까

_____

10 그는 왔 습니까

_____

Step 3 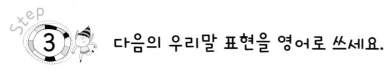 다음의 우리말 표현을 영어로 쓰세요.

1 그녀는 바다에서 수영했습니까?

Did she swim in the sea ?

2 Mike는 이야기를 (a story) 썼습니까?

_____

3 당신은 파스타를 (pasta) 요리했습니까?

_____

4 Billy는 그 열쇠를 (the key) 찾았습니까?

_____

5 그들은 지난 주에 (last week) 스키를 타러 갔습니까?

_____

6 Mary는 당신에게 (you) 전화했습니까?

_____

7 그는 그 나무들을 (the trees) 심었습니까?

_____

8 당신의 엄마와 아빠는 집에 (at home) 머물렀습니까?

_____

9 그녀는 쿠키들을 (cookies) 만들었습니까?

_____

10 그는 그 모임에 (to the meeting) 왔습니까?

_____

A. 빈칸을 채우세요.

English	Korean	English	Korean
call/called			만들다
	오다	plant/planted	
cook/cooked			머물다
find/found			수영하다
	스키를 타러 가다	write/wrote	

B. 빈칸을 채우세요.

1 일반동사 의문문(과거)에 대한 긍정의 대답은 'Yes, 주어 +   .' 로 답한다.

2 일반동사 의문문(과거)에 대한 부정의 대답은 'No, 주어 +   .' 로 답한다.

C. 다음 질문에 대한 대답을 완성하세요.

Q: Did Jack and Suji ride a bike?   A: Yes,   did.

Q: Did your sister buy the boat?   A: No,   didn't.

D. 그림을 보고 주어진 동사를 이용하여 과거형 문장을 완성하세요.

1

2

3

4

Word Box

| write | study | go shopping | make |

1 _____ they _____ a kite?

2 _____ Jane _____ yesterday?

3 _____ Tom _____ a diary?

4 _____ you _____ math?

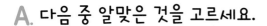

A. 다음 중 알맞은 것을 고르세요.

1 Linda (visits / visited) her grandparents yesterday.

2 They (swim / swam) in the sea last week.

3 We (studyed / studied) for the exam.

4 It (rained / rainned) a lot.

B. 다음 중 알맞은 것을 고르세요.

1 My mom bought (a dish / an dish) yesterday.

2 Jay gave (a orange / an orange) to me.

3 I didn't eat (a sandwich / an sandwich) in the morning.

4 Did you see (a ant / an ant) on the ground?

C. 다음 질문에 대한 대답을 완성하세요.

1 Q: Did your brother go skating?   A: Yes, _____

2 Q: Did the kids eat dinner?   A: Yes, _____

3 Q: Did Jenny ride a bicycle?   A: No, _____

4 Q: Did you (당신들) watch the soccer game?

A: Yes, _____

D. 주어진 단어를 사용하여 문장을 완성하세요.

1 went / he / yesterday / to the park / .

   _____

2 did / play / you / the violin / ?

   _____

3 snow / did / it / ?

   _____

4 didn't / I / last week / work / .

   _____

E. 다음 문장을 영작하세요.

1 그들은 상자들을 날랐다. (carry, boxes)

   _____

2 내 아빠는 자동차를 운전하지 않았다. (drive, a car)

   _____

3 그 아기는 어제 밤에 울었습니까? (cry, last night)

   _____

4 나는 동물원에서 코끼리들을 보지 못했다. (see, at the zoo)

   _____

be going to 긍정문

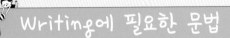

① be going to 긍정문의 형태

주어	be going to	동사원형
I	am going to	
You / They / We	are going to	exercise.
He / She / It	is going to	

② be going to 긍정문 맛보기

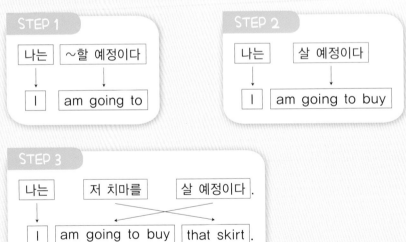

STEP 1

나는	~할 예정이다

I	am going to

STEP 2

나는	살 예정이다

I	am going to buy

STEP 3

나는	저 치마를	살 예정이다 .

I	am going to buy	that skirt .

③ be going to 긍정문의 쓰임

예문	해석
They are going to buy that car.	
We are going to watch the movie tonight.	~할 예정이다
It is going to rain.	

* be going to vs. will

	be going to	will
쓰임	미래에 일어날 일에 대해 이야기할 때 사용하며 뒤에 동사원형이 온다.	
	계획이 있는 가까운 미래의 일에 대해 사용	말하는 사람의 의지나 의견이 많이 들어간 경우와 방금 결정한 일에 대해 사용
예문	We're going to see the movie tonight. (오늘 밤에 우리는 그 영화를 볼 예정이다.)	I will have orange juice. (나는 오렌지 주스를 마실게요.) I will study hard for the test. (나는 그 시험을 대비해 공부를 열심히 할 것이다.)

Writing에 필요한 문법 확인

A. 다음 중 알맞은 것을 고르세요.

1 I am going to (play / plays) with my dog.

2 You (am / are / is) going to buy a bag.

3 Anne will (write / writes) a book.

4 They will (help / helps) the old people.

5 We (am / are / is) going to cook pasta.

B. <보기>의 단어를 이용하여 문장을 완성하세요.

<보기> learn   eat   swim   paint   give

1 My cat is going to _____ the food. (내 고양이가 그 음식을 먹을 예정이다.)

2 We are going to _____ the wall. (우리는 그 벽을 페인트칠할 예정이다.)

3 I will _____ English. (나는 영어를 배울 것이다.)

4 You are going to _____ after school.
   (당신은 방과 후에 수영을 할 예정이다.)

5 I will _____ you the game player.
   (나는 그 게임 플레이어를 당신에게 줄 것이다.)

C. 주어진 단어를 사용하여 문장을 완성하세요.

1 is going to / clean the house / he / .   _____

2 snow / is going to / it / .   _____

3 play the violin / Eric / is going to / .   _____

4 the girl / read the book / is going to / .   _____

5 sing / are going to / the students / .   _____

D. 다음 중 틀린 부분을 바르게 고치세요.

1 You is going to eat dinner.   _____

2 I am going to makes sandwiches.   _____

3 Mom is going to cleans the room.   _____

4 They am going to study math.   _____

5 Rob is going to takes a nap.   _____

Word List

English	Korean	English	Korean
animal	동물	help	돕다
bake	굽다	music	음악
buy	사다	painting	그림
enjoy	즐기다	travel	여행하다
fix	고치다, 수리하다	world	세계

 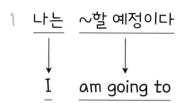 다음의 우리말 표현을 영어로 쓰세요.

1 나는   ~할 예정이다
   ↓   ↓
   I   am going to

2 Ashley는   ~할 예정이다
_____

3 그들은   ~할 예정이다
_____

4 우리는   ~할 예정이다
_____

5 그 소년은 (the boy)   ~할 예정이다
_____

6 그 고양이는 (the cat)   ~할 예정이다
_____

7 우리는   ~할 예정이다
_____

8 Tom 삼촌은 (Uncle Tom)   ~할 예정이다
_____

9 그 학생들은 (the students)   ~할 예정이다
_____

10 당신은   ~할 예정이다
_____

 다음의 우리말 표현을 영어로 쓰세요.

1 <u>나는</u>   <u>살 예정이다</u>
    ↓   ↓
    <u>I</u>   <u>am going to buy</u>

2 Ashley는 고칠 예정이다

_____

3 그들은 먹을 예정이다

_____

4 우리는 볼 (see) 예정이다

_____

5 그 소년은 즐길 예정이다

_____

6 그 고양이는 놀 (play) 예정이다

_____

7 우리는 도울 예정이다

_____

8 Tom 삼촌은 구울 예정이다

_____

9 그 학생들은 연주할 (play) 예정이다

_____

10 당신은 여행할 예정이다

_____

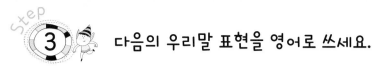

Step 3 다음의 우리말 표현을 영어로 쓰세요.

1   나는   저 치마를   살 예정이다.

I am going to buy   that skirt .

2   Ashley는   그녀의 컴퓨터를 (her computer) 고칠 예정이다.

_____

3   그들은   피자를 (pizza) 먹을 예정이다.

_____

4   우리는   콘서트를 (a concert) 볼 예정이다.

_____

5   그 소년은   그 그림들을 (the paintings) 즐길 예정이다.

_____

6   그 고양이는   그녀의 엄마와 함께 (with her mom) 놀 예정이다.

_____

7   우리는   그 동물들을 (the animals) 도울 예정이다.

_____

8   Tom 삼촌은   케이크를 (a cake) 구울 예정이다.

_____

9   그 학생들은   음악을   연주할 예정이다.

_____

10   당신은   세계를 (the world) 여행할 예정이다.

_____

A. 빈칸을 채우세요.

English	Korean	English	Korean
	동물		돕다
bake			음악
	사다	painting	
enjoy			여행하다
	고치다, 수리하다	world	

B. 빈칸을 채우세요.

1   와   은 미래에 일어날 일에 대해 이야기한다.

2 'be going to'와 'will'의 뒤에는   이 온다.

3 말하는 사람의 의지가 많이 들어간 경우에는   을 사용한다.

4 계획이 있는 가까운 미래의 일에 대해서는   를 사용한다.

C. 그림을 보고 be going to와 주어진 단어를 사용하여 문장을 완성하세요.

1

Sean

2

Sky   Eric

3

Ben

4

Sarah

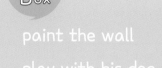
Word Box

paint the wall   take a nap

play with his dog   read the book

1 Sean _____ .

2 Eric and Sky _____ .

3 Ben _____ .

4 Sarah _____ .

be going to 부정문

Writing에 필요한 문법

① be going to 부정문의 형태

be going to 부정형: be동사 뒤에 not을 붙인다.

주어	be going to 부정형	동사원형
I	am not going to	
You / We / They	are not(aren't) going to	play.
He / She / It	is not(isn't) going to	

② be going to 부정문 맛보기

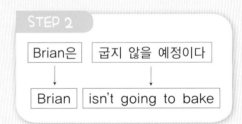

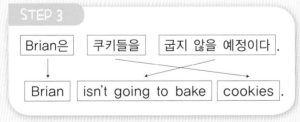

③ be going to 부정문의 쓰임

예문	해석
They are not going to walk to school. Sean is not going to study after school.	~하지 않을 예정이다

66

	be going to + 동사원형	be going to + 장소
해석	~할 예정이다	~에 가는 중이다
예문	They are going to study math. (그들은 수학을 공부할 예정이다.)	We are going to the library. (우리는 도서관에 가는 중이다.)

Writing에 필요한 문법 확인

A. be going to의 뜻이 다른 문장에 동그라미 하세요.

1 I am going to exercise.

2 My brother is going to study.

3 Mom is going to the bookstore.

4 The cat is going to eat.

5 It is going to rain.

B. 괄호 안의 단어가 들어갈 위치에 V 하세요.

1 He is going to sleep. (not)

2 The computer is going to work. (not)

3 I am going to play in the rain. (not)

4 They are going to drive to school. (not)

5 We are going to enjoy the movie. (not)

C. 다음 중 틀린 부분을 바르게 고치세요.

1 You is going to the library.　　　　_____

2 I not am going to make lunch.　　　_____

3 The baby is not going to sleeps.　　_____

4 They are not going to plays.　　　　_____

5 My grandma are not going to visit us.　_____

D. 다음 문장을 부정문으로 바꿔 쓰세요.

1 I'm going to watch TV.

_____

2 Dad is going to water the plants.

_____

3 We are going to play music.

_____

4 Justin is going to clean his room.

_____

5 They are going to fix their table.

_____

Word List

English	Korean	English	Korean
ask	질문하다, 묻다	there	거기에
climb	오르다	mountain	산
cookie	쿠키	wall	벽
snow	눈이 오다	wash	닦다, 씻다
take the bus	버스를 타다	question	질문

step 1 다음의 우리말 표현을 영어로 쓰세요.

1. Brian은   ~하지 않을 예정이다

     ↓   ↓

   Brian   isn't going to

2. Jen은   ~하지 않을 예정이다

_____

3. 나는   ~하지 않을 예정이다

_____

4. 그들은   ~하지 않을 예정이다

_____

5. 그 소녀는 (the girl)   ~하지 않을 예정이다

_____

6. 아빠는 (Dad)   ~하지 않을 예정이다

_____

7. 날씨가 (it)   ~하지 않을 예정이다

_____

8. 당신은   ~하지 않을 예정이다

_____

9. 그들은   ~하지 않을 예정이다

_____

10. 우리는   ~하지 않을 예정이다

_____

 **다음의 우리말 표현을 영어로 쓰세요.**

1 <u>Brian은</u> <u>굽지 않을 예정이다</u>

   ↓   ↓

   <u>Brian</u> <u>isn't going to bake</u>

2 Jen은 타지 (take) 않을 예정이다

_____

3 나는 물어보지 않을 예정이다

_____

4 그들은 오르지 않을 예정이다

_____

5 그 소녀는 페인트칠하지 (paint) 않을 예정이다

_____

6 아빠는 닦지 않을 예정이다

_____

7 눈이 오지 않을 예정이다

_____

8 당신은 가지 (go) 않을 예정이다

_____

9 그들은 사지 (buy) 않을 예정이다

_____

10 우리는 (운동 경기를) 하지 (play) 않을 예정이다

_____

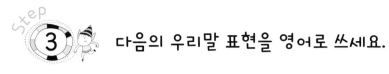

3 다음의 우리말 표현을 영어로 쓰세요.

1 Brian은 쿠키들을 굽지 않을 예정이다.

Brian isn't going to bake cookies .

2 Jen은 버스를 (the bus) 타지 않을 예정이다.

_____

3 나는 어떤 질문들도 (any questions) 물어보지 않을 예정이다.

_____

4 그들은 그 산을 (the mountain) 오르지 않을 예정이다.

_____

5 그 소녀는 그 벽을 (the wall) 페인트칠하지 않을 예정이다.

_____

6 아빠는 그의 차를 (his car) 닦지 않을 예정이다.

_____

7 부산에 (in Busan) 눈이 오지 않을 예정이다.

_____

8 당신은 거기에 (there) 가지 않을 예정이다.

_____

9 그들은 그 트럭을 (the truck) 사지 않을 예정이다.

_____

10 우리는 야구를 (baseball) 하지 않을 예정이다.

_____

A. 빈칸을 채우세요.

English	Korean	English	Korean
ask			거기에
	오르다	mountain	
cookie		wall	
	눈이 오다		닦다, 씻다
take the bus		question	

B. 빈칸을 채우세요.

1 'be going to + 장소'는   라는 뜻을 가진다.

2 'be going to + 동사원형'은   라는 뜻을 가진다.

C. 다음 문장을 완성하세요.

1 I _____ the mall.
　(나는 그 쇼핑몰에 가는 중이다.)

2 Tom _____ the museum.
　(Tom은 그 박물관에 가는 중이다.)

3 They _____ math.
　(그들은 수학을 공부할 예정이다.)

D. 그림을 보고 be going to와 주어진 단어를 사용하여 부정문을 완성하세요.

1  Joe

2  Summer

3

4

Word Box

rain   fix their car   watch TV   water the plants

1 Joe _____ .

2 Summer _____ .

3 Mom and Dad _____ .

4 It _____ .

Lesson 3   be going to 의문문

Writing에 필요한 문법

① be going to 의문문의 형태

be동사	주어	going to	동사원형
Am	I		
Are	you / they / we	going to	play?
Is	he / she / it		

② be going to 의문문 맛보기

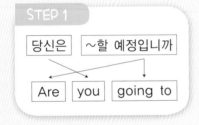

STEP 1

| 당신은 | ~할 예정입니까 |

| Are | you | going to |

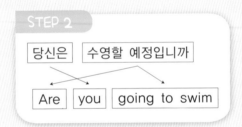

STEP 2

| 당신은 | 수영할 예정입니까 |

| Are | you | going to swim |

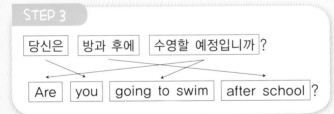

STEP 3

| 당신은 | 방과 후에 | 수영할 예정입니까? |

| Are | you | going to swim | after school ? |

③ be going to 의문문의 쓰임

예문	해석
Q: Are they going to watch TV? A: Yes, they are. / No, they aren't.	~할 예정입니까?
Q: Is Mina going to sleep? A: Yes, she is / No, she isn't.	

＊ 전치사와 전치사구

	전치사	전치사구: 전치사 + 명사
쓰임	명사 앞에 위치	주로 문장에서 뒤에 위치
예시	in, at, with, about, after 등	at night, in the room, before the movie 등
예문	Meet me at the mall. I study English with Mom. Can we play after 12 o'clock?	I am going to exercise after school. Are the boys going to swim in the afternoon? Are you going to buy that dress in the window?

Writing에 필요한 문법 확인

A. 전치사구가 있는 문장에 동그라미 하세요.

1 The rabbits are going to run.

2 We are going to play a game.

3 You are going to study after school.

4 Are they going to do homework?

5 Are you going to take the bus in the morning?

B. 다음 문장에서 전치사구에 동그라미 하세요.

1 I am going to play in my room.

2 Are you going to watch TV at night?

3 It is going to snow this afternoon.

4 Are they going to play soccer at the playground?

5 We are going to the museum near your house.

C. 다음 중 알맞은 것을 고르세요.

1 (Am / Are / Is) the horse going to run?

2 (Am / Are / Is) you going to brush your teeth?

3 (Am / Are / Is) I going to win the race?

4 (Am / Are / Is) Gina going to study?

5 (Am / Are / Is) the students going to the library?

D. 다음 문장을 의문문으로 바꿔 쓰세요.

1 The girl is going to have ice cream.

_____

2 They are going to climb the mountain.

_____

3 Justin is going to make dinner.

_____

4 The flowers are going to fall.

_____

5 The dog is going to catch the ball.

_____

Word List

English	Korean	English	Korean
after school	방과 후에	kitten	아기고양이
at night	밤에	plant	식물
catch	잡다	race	경주, 달리기
food	음식	this afternoon	오늘 오후에
house	집	water	(식물 등에) 물을 주다

 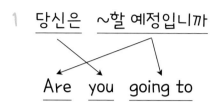 다음의 우리말 표현을 영어로 쓰세요.

1 당신은　~할 예정입니까

　　Are　you　going to

2 그 소년은 (the boy)　~할 예정입니까

　　_____

3 우리는　~할 예정입니까

　　_____

4 Cathy는　~할 예정입니까

　　_____

5 당신들은　~할 예정입니까

　　_____

6 아빠는 (Dad)　~할 예정입니까

　　_____

7 그들은　~할 예정입니까

　　_____

8 그 아기고양이는　~할 예정입니까

　　_____

9 그는　~할 예정입니까

　　_____

10 당신은　~할 예정입니까

　　_____

 **다음의 우리말 표현을 영어로 쓰세요.**

1 <u>당신은</u> <u>수영할 예정입니까</u>

   <u>Are</u> <u>you</u> <u>going to swim</u>

2 그 소년은 잡을 예정입니까

   _____

3 우리는 살 (buy) 예정입니까

   _____

4 Cathy는 물을 줄 예정입니까

   _____

5 당신들은 (운동 경기)를 할 (play) 예정입니까

   _____

6 아빠는 고칠 (fix) 예정입니까

   _____

7 그들은 달릴 (run) 예정입니까

   _____

8 그 아기고양이는 먹을 예정입니까

   _____

9 그는 글을 쓸 (write) 예정입니까

   _____

10 당신은 운동할 (exercise) 예정입니까

   _____

Step **3** 다음의 우리말 표현을 영어로 쓰세요.

1 당신은 방과 후에 수영할 예정입니까?

Are you going to swim after school ?

2 그 소년은 그 공을 (the ball) 잡을 예정입니까?

_____

3 우리는 그 집을 (the house) 살 예정입니까?

_____

4 Cathy는 그 식물들에 (the plants) 물을 줄 예정입니까?

_____

5 당신들은 축구를 (soccer) 할 예정입니까?

_____

6 아빠는 그 프린터를 (the printer) 고칠 예정입니까?

_____

7 그들은 경주에서 (in the race) 달릴 예정입니까?

_____

8 그 아기고양이는 그 음식을 (the food) 먹을 예정입니까?

_____

9 그는 밤에 글을 쓸 예정입니까?

_____

10 당신은 오늘 오후에 운동할 예정입니까?

_____

A. 빈칸을 채우세요.

English	Korean	English	Korean
after school		kitten	
	밤에		식물
catch		race	
	음식		오늘 오후에
house			(식물 등에) 물을 주다

B. 빈칸을 채우세요.

1 '전치사 + 명사'를   라고 부른다.

2 사람이나 사물에 이름을 붙인 것을   라고 한다.

3 전치사구는 주로 문장에서   에 위치한다.

C. 다음 문장에서 전치사구에 동그라미 하세요.

1 Are you going to buy that dress in the window?

2 I am going to exercise after school.

3 Are the boys going to swim in the afternoon?

80

D. 그림을 보고 be going to와 주어진 단어를 사용하여 의문문을 완성하세요.

1

2

Cathy

3

4

Gary

Word Box

fall   do homework   take the bus   catch the ball

1 _____ the dog _____?

2 _____ Cathy _____ in the morning?

3 _____ the flowers _____?

4 _____ Gary _____?

A. 주어진 단어를 사용하여 문장을 완성하세요.

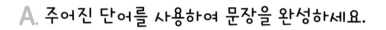

am going to   are going to   is going to

1 I _____ walk to school.

2 Tom _____ cook.

3 You _____ read.

4 They _____ eat pizza.

5 Uncle Sean _____ play music.

B. 다음 문장을 완성하세요.

1 I _____ the mall.
   (나는 그 쇼핑몰에 가는 중이다.)

2 Tom _____ the museum.
   (Tom은 그 박물관에 가는 중이다.)

3 We are going to _____ soccer.
   (그들은 축구를 할 예정이다.)

4 I _____ have orange juice.
   (나는 오렌지 주스를 마실게요.)

5 You will _____ hard for the test.
   (당신은 그 시험을 대비해 공부를 열심히 할 것이다.)

C. 다음 문장을 부정문으로 바꿔 쓰세요.

1 Brian is going to bake cookies.

   _____

2 They are going to climb the mountain.

   _____

3 I'm going to go there.

   _____

4 The boy is going to paint.

   _____

D. 다음 문장을 영작하세요.

1 당신은 세계를 여행할 예정이다. (travel the world)

   _____

2 아빠는 그의 차를 닦지 않을 예정이다. (wash his car)

   _____

3 그가 밤에 글을 쓸 예정입니까? (at night)

   _____

4 우리가 콘서트를 볼 예정입니까? (see a concert)

   _____

Unit 4

Lesson 1

There be 긍정문

① There be 긍정문의 형태

There	be 동사	명사	
There	is	an apple	on the table.
	are	apples	

② There be 긍정문 맛보기

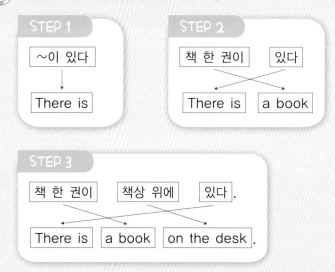

STEP 1

~이 있다

↓

There is

STEP 2

책 한 권이   있다

There is   a book

STEP 3

책 한 권이   책상 위에   있다 .

There is   a book   on the desk .

③ There be 긍정문의 쓰임

쓰임	예문	해석
주로 장소 표현과 함께 존재를 나타낼 때	There is a boy under the tree.	~이/가 있다
	There are books in the backpack.	~들이 있다

- 명사가 하나일 때에는 그 앞에 a/an을 붙인다.
- 명사가 두 개 이상일 때는 대부분의 명사에 s를 붙인다.
  (예시) a girl — two girls   a book — two books
         an orange — two oranges
- -s/-sh/-ch/-x로 끝나는 명사는 두 개 이상일 때 명사에 es를 붙인다.
  (예시) a bus — two buses   a dish — two dishes
         a church — two churches   a fox — two foxes

* milk, water, juice 등 셀 수 없는 명사는 그 앞에 a/an을 붙이지 않는다.
  (예시) ✗ milk   ✗ milk ✗   milk   ✗ water   ✗ water ✗   water

Writing에 필요한 문법 확인

A. 다음 중 알맞은 것을 고르세요.

1   I have two (apple / apples).

2   Gina bought (a pencil / a pencils).

3   We made many (cookie / cookies).

4   She gave (water / waters) to me.

5   Do you want (a juice / juice)?

B. 다음 중 알맞은 것을 고르세요.

1   (The girls / The girles) are singing a song.

2   The man carried (boxs / boxes).

3   I love (dogs / doges) and cats.

4   Pam drinks (milk / milks) for breakfast.

5   She has two (hats / hates).

C. 다음 중 알맞은 것을 고르세요.

1 There (is / are) many books on the desk.

2 There (is / are) two chairs in the room.

3 There (is / are) a girl in the house.

4 There (is / are) water in the cup.

5 There (is / are) cookies on the dish.

D. There be를 사용하여 문장을 완성하세요.

1 _____ a desk in my room.

2 _____ apples in the box.

3 _____ many kids in the classroom.

4 _____ milk in the bottle.

5 _____ an orange on the table.

Word List

English	Korean	English	Korean
clock/clocks	(벽에 거는) 시계	rose/roses	장미꽃
egg/eggs	달걀	sandwich/ sandwiches	샌드위치
glass/glasses	유리잔	student/students	학생
pencil/pencils	연필	tiger/tigers	호랑이
playground/ playgrounds	운동장	wall/walls	벽

 다음의 우리말 표현을 영어로 쓰세요.

1 ~이 있다

↓

There is

2 ~가 있다

_____

3 ~들이 있다

_____

4 ~이 있다

_____

5 ~들이 있다

_____

6 ~가 있다

_____

7 ~들이 있다

_____

8 ~들이 있다

_____

9 ~가 있다

_____

10 ~들이 있다

_____

다음의 우리말 표현을 영어로 쓰세요.

1 책 한 권이   있다

There is a book

2 벽시계 하나가   있다

_____

3 샌드위치들이   있다

_____

4 약간의 물이 (some water)   있다

_____

5 연필들이   있다

_____

6 약간의 우유가 (some milk)   있다

_____

7 학생들이   있다

_____

8 장미꽃들이   있다

_____

9 호랑이 한 마리가   있다

_____

10 달걀들이   있다

_____

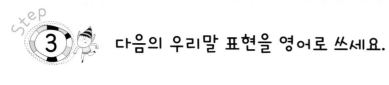

3 다음의 우리말 표현을 영어로 쓰세요.

1 책 한 권이 책상 위에 있다.

  There is a book on the desk .

2 벽시계 하나가 벽에 (on the wall) 있다.

  _____

3 샌드위치들이 탁자 위에 (on the table) 있다.

  _____

4 약간의 물이 컵에 (in the cup) 있다.

  _____

5 연필들이 책상 위에 (on the desk) 있다.

  _____

6 약간의 우유가 유리잔에 (in the glass) 있다.

  _____

7 학생들이 운동장에 (at the playground) 있다.

  _____

8 장미꽃들이 정원에 (in the garden) 있다.

  _____

9 호랑이 한 마리가 동물원에 (in the zoo) 있다.

  _____

10 달걀들이 바구니에 (in the basket) 있다.

  _____

A. 빈칸을 채우세요.

English	Korean	English	Korean
clock/clocks			장미꽃
egg/eggs			샌드위치
	유리잔	student/students	
	연필	tiger/tigers	
playground/playgrounds			벽

B. 빈칸을 채우세요.

1 명사가 하나일 때는 그 앞에 _____ 을 붙인다.

2 명사가 두 개 이상일 때는 대부분의 명사에 _____ 를 붙인다.

3 -s/-sh/-ch/-x로 끝나는 명사는 두 개 이상일 때 명사에 _____ 를 붙인다.

C. 주어진 단어를 이용하여 문장을 완성하세요.

1 There are many _____ on the street. (bus)

2 There is some _____ in the glass. (water)

3 There is _____ on the table. (egg)

4 There are _____ in the zoo. (animal)

D. 그림을 보고 There be와 주어진 단어를 이용하여 문장을 완성하세요.

1

2

3

4

Word Box

book   doll   some water   banana

1 _____ in the box.

2 _____ in the basket.

3 _____ in the glass.

4 _____ on the desk.

There be 부정문

Writing에 필요한 문법

1 There be 부정문의 형태

주어에 따라 모양이 달라진다.

There	be동사 부정형		명사	
There	is not(isn't)	(any)	juice	in the refrigerator.
	are not(aren't)		apples	

2 There be 부정문 맛보기

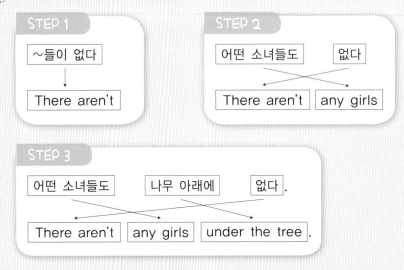

STEP 1

| ~들이 없다 |
| ↓ |
| There aren't |

STEP 2

| 어떤 소녀들도 | 없다 |
| There aren't | any girls |

STEP 3

| 어떤 소녀들도 | 나무 아래에 | 없다 . |
| There aren't | any girls | under the tree . |

3 There be 부정문의 쓰임

예문	해석
There isn't(any) water in the glass.	어떤 ~도 없다
There aren't(any) apples in the basket.	어떤 ~들도 없다

* There be 구문은 주로 장소를 표현하는 전치사와 함께 쓰인다.

- 장소를 표현하는 전치사

전치사	의미	전치사	의미
in	~안에	near	~근처에
on	~위에	next to	~옆에
under	~아래에	in front of	~앞에
behind	~뒤에	between A and B	A와 B 사이에

Writing에 필요한 문법 확인

A. 다음 중 알맞은 것을 고르세요.

1　There is some milk (in / on) the glass.

2　There are books (in / on) the table.

3　There is a bench (under / in) the tree.

4　There is a house (on / behind) the school.

5　There are many cars (under / in) the city.

B. 알맞은 전치사를 넣어 문장을 완성하세요.

1　There is a church ＿＿＿＿＿＿＿ the school and the house.
　(학교와 집 사이에)

2　There are girls ＿＿＿＿＿＿＿ the tree. (나무 뒤에)

3　There is a backpack ＿＿＿＿＿＿＿ the desk. (책상 옆에)

4　My house is ＿＿＿＿＿＿＿ the church. (교회 앞에)

5　The shop is ＿＿＿＿＿＿＿ the bus stop. (버스 정류장 근처에)

C. 괄호 안의 단어가 들어갈 위치에 V 하세요.

1 There any juice in the bottle. (isn't)

2 There are any flowers in the garden. (not)

3 There are any cars on the street. (not)

4 There any chairs in the room. (aren't)

5 There any salt in the kitchen. (isn't)

D. any를 사용하여 다음 문장을 부정문으로 바꿔 쓰세요.

1 There are balls on the ground.

_____

2 There are snacks in the kitchen.

_____

3 There is water in the bottle.

_____

4 There are trees behind the house.

_____

5 There are flowers in the vase.

_____

Word List

English	Korean	English	Korean
ball/balls	공	river/rivers	강
bowl/bowls	그릇	skirt/skirts	치마
closet/closets	옷장	soup	수프
hat/hats	모자	store/stores	상점
refrigerator/ refrigerators	냉장고	town/towns	마을

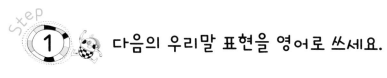

Step 1 · 다음의 우리말 표현을 영어로 쓰세요.

1 ~들이 없다
↓
There aren't
_____

2 ~들이 없다
_____

3 ~들이 없다
_____

4 ~이 없다
_____

5 ~들이 없다
_____

6 ~들이 없다
_____

7 ~이 없다
_____

8 ~들이 없다
_____

9 ~가 없다
_____

10 ~들이 없다
_____

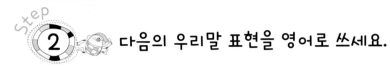

Step **2** 다음의 우리말 표현을 영어로 쓰세요.

1 <u>어떤 소녀들도</u>   <u>없다</u>

<u>There aren't</u>   <u>any girls</u>

2 어떤 공들도   없다

_____

3 어떤 자동차들도   없다

_____

4 어떤 물도   없다

_____

5 어떤 강들도   없다

_____

6 어떤 나무들도   없다

_____

7 어떤 우유도   없다

_____

8 어떤 모자들도   없다

_____

9 어떤 수프도   없다

_____

10 어떤 치마들도   없다

_____

Step 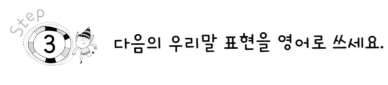 다음의 우리말 표현을 영어로 쓰세요.

1 어떤 소녀들도 나무 아래에 없다.

There aren't any girls under the tree .

2 어떤 공들도 그 상자 안에 없다.

_____

3 어떤 자동차들도 내 집 앞에 없다.

_____

4 어떤 물도 그 냉장고 안에 없다.

_____

5 어떤 강들도 내 마을 근처에 없다.

_____

6 어떤 나무들도 그 학교 옆에 없다.

_____

7 어떤 우유도 그 유리잔에 (in the glass) 없다.

_____

8 어떤 모자들도 그 상점 안에 없다.

_____

9 어떤 수프도 그 그릇 안에 없다.

_____

10 어떤 치마들도 그 옷장 안에 없다.

_____

A. 빈칸을 채우세요.

English	Korean	English	Korean
	공	river/rivers	
bowl/bowls			치마
	옷장	soup	
hat/hats			상점
	냉장고	town/towns	

B. 빈칸을 채우세요.

전치사	의미	전치사	의미
	~안에		~근처에
	~위에		~옆에
	~아래에		~앞에
	~뒤에		A와B 사이에

C. 그림을 보고 주어진 단어를 이용하여 There be 부정문을 완성하세요.

1

2

3

4

Word Box

picture   tree   water   toy

1 _____ in front of the house.

2 _____ in the box.

3 _____ on the wall.

4 _____ in the cup.

Unit 4
Lesson 3

There be 의문문

Writing에 필요한 문법

① There be 의문문의 형태

be동사	there	명사	
Is	there	an egg	in the refrigerator?
Are		eggs	

② There be 의문문 맛보기

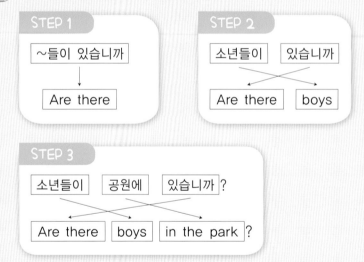

STEP 1

~들이 있습니까
↓
Are there

STEP 2

소년들이 있습니까
Are there boys

STEP 3

소년들이 공원에 있습니까?
Are there boys in the park?

③ There be 의문문의 쓰임

예문	해석
Is there a store behind the house?	~이/가 있습니까?
Are there flowers in the garden?	~들이 있습니까?

* There be 의문문에 대한 대답

‒ 'Is there ~?'의 물음에 긍정이면 'Yes, there is.'로, 부정이면 'No, there isn't.'로 대답한다.

(예문) Q: Is there a piano in your house?

    A: Yes, there is. / No, there isn't.

‒ 'Are there ~?'의 물음에 긍정이면 'Yes, there are.'로, 부정이면 'No, there aren't.'로 대답한다.

(예문) Q: Are there many desks in the classroom?

    A: Yes, there are. / No, there aren't.

Writing에 필요한 문법 확인

A. 알맞은 대답에 동그라미 하세요.

1 Q: Is there a pencil on the desk?

  A: (Yes, there is. / No, it isn't.)

2 Q: Are there many animals in the zoo?

  A: (Yes, there is. / Yes, there are.)

3 Q: Is there some milk in the glass?

  A: (Yes, it is. / No, there isn't.)

4 Q: Are there oranges on the dish?

  A: (No, there aren't. / No, there isn't.)

5 Q: Is there a clock on the wall?

  A: (Yes, there is. / No, there aren't.)

B. 다음 질문과 대답을 완성하세요.

1 Q: _____ there many cookies?   A: _____, there aren't.

2 Q: _____ there a book on the desk? A: _____, there is.

3 Q: Is there water in the bottle?   A: Yes, _____.

4 Q: Are there students in the classroom? A: No, _____.

5 Q: Is there a cup on the table?   A: No, _____.

C. 다음 문장을 의문문으로 바꿔 쓰세요.

1 There is a bicycle on the street.

_____

2 There are snacks in the kitchen.

_____

3 There is a house next to the school.

_____

4 There are cars behind the tree.

_____

D. 주어진 단어를 사용하여 문장을 완성하세요.

1 is / a book / there / under the table / ?

_____

2 in the sky / are / stars / there / ?

_____

3 juice / there / is / in the glass / ?

_____

4 on the grass / any girls / there / are / ?

_____

Word List

English	Korean	English	Korean
bank/banks	은행	on stage	무대 위에
bottle/bottles	병	post office/post offices	우체국
letter/letters	편지	shelf/shelves	책꽂이, 선반
mailbox/mailboxes	우편함	singer/singers	가수
man/men	남자	star/stars	별

 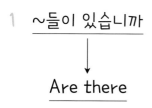 **다음의 우리말 표현을 영어로 쓰세요.**

1 <u>~들이 있습니까</u>

　　↓

　<u>Are there</u>

2 ~가 있습니까

_____

3 ~들이 있습니까

_____

4 ~가 있습니까

_____

5 ~가 있습니까

_____

6 ~들이 있습니까

_____

7 ~가 있습니까

_____

8 ~들이 있습니까

_____

9 ~가 있습니까

_____

10 ~들이 있습니까

_____

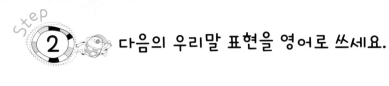

Step **2** 다음의 우리말 표현을 영어로 쓰세요.

1 소년들이 있습니까

Are there boys

2 주스가 있습니까

_____

3 책들이 있습니까

_____

4 아기가 있습니까

_____

5 은행이 있습니까

_____

6 편지들이 있습니까

_____

7 남자가 있습니까

_____

8 별들이 있습니까

_____

9 우체국이 있습니까

_____

10 가수들이 있습니까

_____

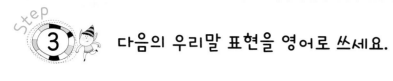 다음의 우리말 표현을 영어로 쓰세요.

1 소년들이 공원에 있습니까?

Are there boys in the park?

2 주스가 그 병 안에 있습니까?

_____

3 책들이 그 책꽃이 위에 있습니까?

_____

4 아기가 그 침대 위에 있습니까?

_____

5 은행이 당신의 집 근처에 있습니까?

_____

6 편지들이 그 우편함 안에 있습니까?

_____

7 남자가 그 나무 옆에 있습니까?

_____

8 별들이 하늘에 (in the sky) 있습니까?

_____

9 우체국이 그 식당 뒤에 (behind the restaurant) 있습니까?

_____

10 가수들이 무대 위에 있습니까?

_____

A. 빈칸을 채우세요.

English	Korean	English	Korean
	은행	on stage	무대 위에
	병	post office/ post offices	
letter/letters		shelf/shelves	
mailbox/ mailboxes			가수
	남자	star/stars	

B. 빈칸을 채우세요.

1 'Is there ~?'의 물음에 긍정이면 'Yes, _____.'로,

부정이면 'No, _____.'로 대답한다.

2 'Are there ~?'의 물음에 긍정이면 'Yes, _____.'로,

부정이면 'No, _____.'로 대답한다.

C. 다음 질문에 대한 대답을 완성하세요.

Q: Is there a baby in the room?　　A: Yes, _____.

Q: Are there snacks on the table?　　A: No, _____.

D. 그림을 보고 주어진 단어를 이용하여 There be 의문문을 완성하세요.

1

2

3

4

Word Box

| coffee | cookie | kid | pencil |

1 _____ in the cup?

2 _____ at the playground?

3 _____ on the dish?

4 _____ between the book and the backpack?

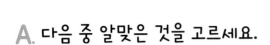
A. 다음 중 알맞은 것을 고르세요.

1 There is (a / an) orange in the refrigerator.

2 Are there any (clocks / clockes) on the wall?

3 There (is / are) a fan on the desk.

4 There aren't any (foxs / foxes) in the zoo.

B. 알맞은 전치사를 넣어 문장을 완성하세요.

1 There aren't any cats _____ the table. (탁자 아래에)

2 There are flowers _____ my house. (나의 집 근처에)

3 There is a boy _____ the tree. (나무 뒤에)

4 There aren't any buses _____ the school. (학교 옆에)

C. 다음 질문에 대한 대답을 완성하세요.

1 Q: Are there books on the shelf?   A: Yes, _____.

2 Q: Is there juice in the glass?   A: No, _____.

3 Q: Is there a fish in the bowl?   A: Yes, _____.

4 Q: Are there many pants in the store? A: No, _____.

D. 주어진 단어를 사용하여 문장을 완성하세요.

1 are / in the classroom / students / there / .

   _____

2 aren't / there / any dogs / in the house / .

   _____

3 any benches / are / in the park / there / ?

   _____

4 on stage / there / any dancers / aren't / .

   _____

E. 다음 문장을 영작하세요.

1 사진이 탁자 위에 있다. (a picture, on the table)

   _____

2 어떤 자켓들도 옷장에 없다. (any jackets, in the closet)

   _____

3 유리 잔에 물이 있습니까? (water, in the glass)

   _____

4 자동차들이 집 앞에 있습니까? (cars, in front of the house)

   _____

Unit 1
Lesson 1 be동사 긍정문(과거)

 Writing에 필요한 문법 확인

A. 1 I was (very) small.
  2 This book was (too) difficult.
  3 The boy was (really) good.
  4 The kids were (so) cute.
  5 You were (very) brave.

B. 1 was 2 were 3 was 4 were
  5 was

C. 1 My teacher was very good.
  2 The cows were thirsty.
  3 The house was very nice.
  4 My friends were smart.
  5 The sky was very blue.

D. 1 The box was heavy.
  2 Dad was very busy.
  3 They were angry.
  4 The birds were fast.
  5 The test was difficult.

[Step 1]
2 I was
3 The book was
4 The cats were
5 The flowers were
6 Mom was
7 The movie was
8 Rob was
9 The students were
10 We were

[Step 2]
2 I was angry
3 The book was here
4 The cats were fast
5 The flowers were beautiful
6 Mom was tired
7 The movie was fun
8 Rob was late
9 The students were ready
10 We were excited

[Step 3]
2 I was angry at you .
3 The book was here yesterday .
4 The cats were really fast.
5 The flowers were so beautiful.
6 Mom was tired after work .
7 The movie was very fun.
8 Rob was late for school .
9 The students were ready for the test .
10 We were excited about the trip .

Unit 1. Lesson 1
Quiz Time
A.

English	Korean	English	Korean
after work	퇴근 후	late	늦은
angry	화난	ready	준비된
excited	신이 난	thirsty	목이 마른
here	여기에	tired	피곤한
interesting	재미있는, 흥미로운	yesterday	어제

110

B. 1 부사   2 사물

C. 1 She was ⟨very⟩ ⟨beautiful⟩.

  2 The girl was ⟨so⟩ ⟨happy⟩.

  3 The box was ⟨really⟩ ⟨heavy⟩.

D. 1 were baseball players

  2 was small

  3 was nice

  4 were brave

Lesson 2 Unit 1

be동사 부정문(과거)

Writing에 필요한 문법 확인

A. 1 was not   2 was not   3 were not
  4 wasn't   5 weren't

B. 1 interested   2 exciting   3 tired
  4 interesting   5 excited

C. 1 The flowers were ∨ beautiful.

  2 The sky was ∨ clear.

  3 The small bug was ∨ cute.

  4 Dad was ∨ hungry.

  5 The box was ∨ big.

D. 1 was not   2 was not
  3 were not   4 was not
  5 were not

[Step 1]

2 The students were not

3 The book was not

4 My puppy was not

5 Judy was not

6 We were not

7 The food was not

8 My toys were not

9 The coffee was not

10 My boots were not

[Step 2]

2 The students were not happy

3 The book was not interesting

4 My puppy was not tired

5 Judy was not a baseball player

6 We were not excited

7 The food was not delicious

8 My toys were not here

9 The coffee was not hot

10 My boots were not light

[Step 3]

2 The students were not happy about the exam .

3 The book was not very interesting.

4 My puppy was not tired after the play .

5 Judy was not a baseball player in high school .

6 We were not excited about the game .

7 The food at the restaurant was not delicious.

8 My toys were not here yesterday .

9 The coffee was not very hot.

10 My boots were not light in the rain .

Unit 1. Lesson 2

Quiz Time

A.

English	Korean	English	Korean
delicious	맛있는	interesting	흥미로운
exam	시험	light	가벼운
excited	신이 난	puppy	강아지
here	여기에	tired	피곤한
hot	뜨거운	toy	장난감

B. 1 excited

2 interested

3 interesting

4 exciting

C. 1 was not hungry

2 was not big

3 was not clear

4 was not fun

Unit 1

Lesson 3   be동사 의문문(과거)

◀ Writing에 필요한 문법 확인 ▶

A. 1 Was the bird cute?

2 Do you have homework?

3 Were you okay?

4 Do they play soccer after school?

5 Was Sarah sick yesterday?

B. 1 Was   2 Were   3 Was   4 Were

5 Was

C. 1 he was   2 she was

3 they weren't   4 it was

5 we weren't

D. 1 Was the food delicious?

2 Were they happy?

3 Was the car expensive?

4 Was Rob tired?

5 Was the movie interesting?

[Step 1]

2 Were   they

3 Was   the plate

4 Was   his room

5 Were   the trees

6 Was   her mom

7 Was   the concert

8 Were   the pants

9 Was   your computer

10 Were   you

[Step 2]

2 Were they late

3 Was the plate clean

4 Was his room dirty

5 Were the trees healthy

6 Was her mom sick

7 Was the concert exciting

8 Were the pants expensive

9 Was your computer slow

10 Were you at home

[Step 3]

2 Were they late for school ?

3 Was the plate on the table clean?

4 Was his room quite dirty?

5 Were the trees and flowers healthy?

6 Was her mom very sick?

112

7 Was the concert exciting and fun ?

8 Were the blue pants expensive?

9 Was your computer slow this morning ?

10 Were you at home last night ?

Unit 1. Lesson 3
Quiz Time

A.

English	Korean	English	Korean
at home	집에	healthy	건강한
clean	깨끗한	late	늦은
difficult	어려운	sick	아픈
dirty	더러운	slow	느린
expensive	비싼	tree	나무

B. he, it

C. 1 she   2 he   3 It

D. 1 Was, interesting

   2 Was, sick

   3 Were, angry

   4 Were, late

Unit 1. Check Up

A. 1 Were   2 Was   3 Were

   4 Was   5 Were

B. 1 We were thirsty.

   2 The water was cold.

   3 The sky was very blue.

   4 Dad was busy.

   5 They were baseball players.

C. 1 The house was nice.

   2 The boxes weren't heavy.

   3 The museum was big.

   4 Were the plants healthy?

D. 1 The test was very difficult.

---

2 Were you angry at me?

3 We were excited about the trip.

4 The coffee was not hot.

Unit 2
Lesson 1 일반동사 긍정문(과거)

Writing에 필요한 문법 확인

A. 1 walked   2 dropped   3 played

   4 went   5 read

B.

현재형	과거형	현재형	과거형
run	ran	eat	ate
come	came	see	saw

C. 1 ate   2 stopped   3 played

   4 liked   5 cried

D. 1 Peter read a comic book.

   2 I listened to music.

   3 They stayed at home.

   4 Nancy talked on the phone.

   5 He went to bed at 9 o'clock.

[Step 1]

2 Kelly   showed

3 He   loved

4 The woman   read

5 I   went

6 She   worked

7 They   danced

8 Mr. Kim   opened

9 The girl   ate

10 I   gave

[Step 2]

2 Kelly showed a picture

3 He loved his cat

4 The woman read a newspaper

5 I went to church

6 She worked at the company

7 They danced together

8 Mr. Kim opened a restaurant

9 The girl ate a hamburger

10 I gave a gift

[Step 3]

2 Kelly showed a picture to me .

3 He loved his cat very much .

4 The woman read a newspaper in
   the morning .

5 I went to church last Sunday .

6 She worked at the company
   last year .

7 They danced together at the party .

8 Mr. Kim opened a restaurant last
   week .

9 The girl ate a hamburger for lunch .

10 I gave a gift to my friend .

Unit 2. Lesson 1

Quiz Time

A.

English	Korean	English	Korean
dance/danced	춤을 추다	open/opened	열다
eat/ate	먹다	read/read	읽다
give/gave	주다	show/showed	보여주다
go/went	가다	study/studied	공부하다
love/loved	사랑하다	work/worked	일하다

B. 1 ed   2 d   3 i, ed   4 마지막 자음

C. 1 read   2 moved   3 dropped
   4 watched

Unit 2
Lesson 2 일반동사 부정문(과거)

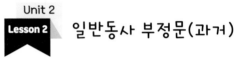

Writing에 필요한 문법 확인

A. 1 girl, cat, car, teacher
   2 ant, umbrella, egg, octopus

B. 1 I didn't eat an apple.
   2 They didn't see a dog.
   3 X
   4 X
   5 He didn't give me an ice cream.

C. 1 didn't   2 didn't   3 go   4 meet
   5 didn't

D. 1 Sunny didn't like milk.
   2 I didn't invite my friends.
   3 He didn't live in Busan.
   4 Karen didn't eat bread for
     breakfast.
   5 We didn't walk to the bus stop.

[Step 1]

2 I didn't

3 Serena didn't

4 My uncle didn't

5 She didn't

6 Jay didn't

7 Mom didn't

8 The boy didn't

9 You didn't

10 The woman didn't

[Step 2]

2 I didn't drink

3 Serena didn't meet

4 My uncle didn't drive

5 She didn't go shopping

6 Jay didn't brush

7 Mom didn't buy

8 The boy didn't smile

9 You didn't close

10 The woman didn't know

[Step 3]

2 I didn't drink coffee .

3 Serena didn't meet her teacher .

4 My uncle didn't drive the truck .

5 She didn't go shopping yesterday .

6 Jay didn't brush his teeth .

7 Mom didn't buy vegetables .

8 The boy didn't smile at me .

9 You didn't close the window .

10 The woman didn't know about the
   fact .

Unit 2. Lesson 2

Quiz Time

A.

English	Korean	English	Korean
brush/brushed	닦다	fix/fixed	고치다
buy/bought	사다	go shopping/went shopping	쇼핑하러 가다
close/closed	닫다	know/knew	알다
drink/drank	마시다	meet/met	만나다
drive/drove	운전하다	smile/smiled	미소 짓다

B. 1 a, an

2 a, e, i, o, u

3 두 개

C. 1 a   2 an   3 an   4 a

D. 1 didn't write

2 didn't listen

3 didn't visit

4 didn't eat

Unit 2
Lesson 3 일반동사 의문문(과거)

Writing에 필요한 문법 확인

A. 1 A: (Yes, he did. / No, she didn't.)

2 A: (Yes, she did. / Yes, she didn't.)

3 A: (No, I did. / No, I didn't.)

4 A: (Yes, they did. / No, we didn't.)

5 A: (Yes, you did. / No, we didn't.)

B. 1 No

2 Yes

3 he didn't

4 it did

5 she didn't

C. 1 Did you drink milk?

2 Did he study English?

3 Did the man help her?

4 Did Jay have dinner?

5 Did she cry yesterday?

D. 1 Did the family have a puppy?

2 Did you buy a jacket?

3 Did Kelly know about him?

4 Did they go to the zoo?

5 Did he live in Seoul?

[Step 1]

2 Did Mike

3 Did you

4 Did Billy

5 Did they

6 Did Mary

7 Did he

8 Did your mom and dad

9 Did she

10 Did he

[Step 2]

2 Did Mike write

3 Did you cook

4 Did Billy find

5 Did they go skiing

6 Did Mary call

7 Did he plant

8 Did your mom and dad stay

9 Did she make

10 Did he come

[Step 3]

2 Did Mike write a story ?

3 Did you cook pasta ?

4 Did Billy find the key ?

5 Did they go skiing last week ?

6 Did Mary call you ?

7 Did he plant the trees ?

8 Did your mom and dad stay at home ?

9 Did she make cookies ?

10 Did he come to the meeting ?

Unit 2. Lesson 3

Quiz Time

A.

English	Korean	English	Korean
call/called	전화하다	make/made	만들다
come/came	오다	plant/planted	심다
cook/cooked	요리하다	stay/stayed	머물다
find/found	찾다	swim/swam	수영하다
go skiing/went skiing	스키를 타러 가다	write/wrote	쓰다

B. 1 did   2 didn't

C. 1 they   2 she

D. 1 Did, make

2 Did, go shopping

3 Did, write

4 Did, study

Unit 2. Check Up

A. 1 visited   2 swam

3 studied   4 rained

B. 1 a dish

2 an orange

3 a sandwich

4 an ant

C. 1 he did

2 they did

3 she didn't

4 we did

D. 1 He went to the park yesterday.

2 Did you play the violin?

3 Did it snow?

4 I didn't work last week.

E. 1 They carried boxes.

2 My dad didn't drive a car.

3 Did the baby cry last night?

4 I didn't see elephants at the zoo.

Unit 3
Lesson 1 be going to 긍정문

Writing에 필요한 문법 확인

A. 1 play   2 are   3 write   4 help
5 are

B. 1 eat   2 paint   3 learn   4 swim
5 give

C. 1 He is going to clean the house.
2 It is going to snow.
3 Eric is going to play the violin.
4 The girl is going to read the book.
5 The students are going to sing.

D. 1 You are going to eat dinner.
2 I am going to make sandwiches.
3 Mom is going to clean the room.
4 They are going to study math.
5 Rob is going to take a nap.

[Step 1]
2 Ashley is going to
3 They are going to
4 We are going to
5 The boy is going to
6 The cat is going to
7 We are going to
8 Uncle Tom is going to
9 The students are going to
10 You are going to

[Step 2]
2 Ashley is going to fix
3 They are going to eat
4 We are going to see
5 The boy is going to enjoy
6 The cat is going to play
7 We are going to help
8 Uncle Tom is going to bake
9 The students are going to play
10 You are going to travel

[Step 3]
2 Ashley is going to fix her computer .
3 They are going to eat pizza .
4 We are going to see a concert .
5 The boy is going to enjoy the paintings .
6 The cat is going to play with her mom .
7 We are going to help the animals .
8 Uncle Tom is going to bake a cake .
9 The students are going to play music .
10 You are going to travel the world .

Unit 3. Lesson 1
Quiz Time

A.

English	Korean	English	Korean
animal	동물	help	돕다
bake	굽다	music	음악
buy	사다	painting	그림
enjoy	즐기다	travel	여행하다
fix	고치다, 수리하다	world	세계

B. 1 be going to, will

2 동사원형   3 will

4 be going to

C. 1 is going to play with his dog

2 are going to paint the wall

3 is going to take a nap

4 is going to read the book

Unit 3
Lesson 2 be going to 부정문

Writing에 필요한 문법 확인

A. 1 I am going to exercise.

2 My brother is going to study.

3 Mom is going to the bookstore.

4 The cat is going to eat.

5 It is going to rain.

B. 1 He is v going to sleep.

2 The computer is v going to work.

3 I am v going to play in the rain.

4 They are v going to drive to school.

5 We are v going to enjoy the movie.

C. 1 You are going to the library.

2 I am not going to make lunch.

3 The baby is not going to sleep.

4 They are not going to play.

5 My grandma is not going to visit us.

D. 1 I'm not going to watch TV.

2 Dad is not going to water the plants.

3 We are not going to play music.

4 Justin is not going to clean his

room.

5 They are not going to fix their table.

[Step 1]

2 Jen is not going to

3 I am not going to

4 They are not going to

5 The girl is not going to

6 Dad is not going to

7 It is not going to

8 You are not going to

9 They are not going to

10 We are not going to

[Step 2]

2 Jen is not going to take

3 I am not going to ask

4 They are not going to climb

5 The girl is not going to paint

6 Dad is not going to wash

7 It is not going to snow

8 You are not going to go

9 They are not going to buy

10 We are not going to play

[Step 3]

2 Jen is not going to take the bus .

3 I am not going to ask any questions .

4 They are not going to climb the mountain .

5 The girl is not going to paint the wall .

6 Dad is not going to wash his car .

7 It is not going to snow in Busan .

8 You are not going to go there .

9 They are not going to buy the truck .

10 We are not going to play baseball .

Unit 3. Lesson 2
Quiz Time

A.

English	Korean	English	Korean
ask	질문하다, 묻다	there	거기에
climb	오르다	mountain	산
cookie	쿠키	wall	벽
snow	눈이 오다	wash	닦다, 씻다
take the bus	버스를 타다	question	질문

B. 1 ~에 가는 중이다

2 ~할 예정이다

C. 1 am going to

2 is going to

3 are going to study

D. 1 isn't going to watch TV

2 isn't going to water the plants

3 aren't going to fix their car

4 isn't going to rain

Unit 3
Lesson 3 be going to 의문문

🖊 Writing에 필요한 문법 확인

A. 1 The rabbits are going to run.

2 We are going to play a game.

3 You are going to study after school.

4 Are they going to do homework?

5 Are you going to take the bus in the morning?

B. 1 I am going to play in my room.

2 Are you going to watch TV at night?

3 It is going to snow this afternoon.

4 Are they going to play soccer at the playground?

5 We are going to the museum near your house.

C. 1 Is   2 Are   3 Am

4 Is   5 Are

D. 1 Is the girl going to have ice cream?

2 Are they going to climb the mountain?

3 Is Justin going to make dinner?

4 Are the flowers going to fall?

5 Is the dog going to catch the ball?

[Step 1]

2 Is the boy going to

3 Are we going to

4 Is Cathy going to

5 Are you going to

6 Is Dad going to

7 Are they going to

8 Is the kitten going to

9 Is he going to

10 Are you going to

[Step 2]

2 Is the boy going to catch

3 Are we going to buy

4 Is Cathy going to water

5 Are you going to play

6 Is Dad going to fix

7 Are they going to run

8 Is the kitten going to eat

9 Is he going to write

10 Are you going to exercise

[Step 3]

2 Is the boy going to catch the ball ?

3 Are we going to buy the house ?

4 Is Cathy going to water the plants ?

5 Are you going to play soccer ?

6 Is Dad going to fix the printer ?

7 Are they going to run in the race ?

8 Is the kitten going to eat the food ?

9 Is he going to write at night ?

10 Are you going to exercise this afternoon ?

Unit 3. Lesson 3

Quiz Time

A.

English	Korean	English	Korean
after school	방과 후에	kitten	아기고양이
at night	밤에	plant	식물
catch	잡다	race	경주, 달리기
food	음식	this afternoon	오늘 오후에
house	집	water	(식물 등에) 물을 주다

B. 1 전치사구   2 명사   3 뒤

C. 1 Are you going to buy that dress in the window?

2 I am going to exercise after school.

3 Are the boys going to swim in the afternoon?

D. 1 Is, going to catch the ball

2 Is, going to take the bus

3 Are, going to fall

4 Is, going to do homework

Unit 3. Check Up

A. 1 am going to   2 is going to

3 are going to   4 are going to

5 is going to

B. 1 am going to   2 is going to

3 play   4 will   5 study

C. 1 Brian is not going to bake cookies.

2 They are not going to climb the mountain.

3 I'm not going to go there.

4 The boy is not going to paint.

D. 1 You are going to travel the world.

2 Dad is not going to wash his car.

3 Is he going to write at night?

4 Are we going to see a concert?

Unit 4

Lesson 1

There be 긍정문

Writing에 필요한 문법 확인

A. 1 apples   2 a pencil

3 cookies   4 water

5 juice

B. 1 The girls   2 boxes

3 dogs   4 milk

5 hats

C. 1 are   2 are   3 is

4 is   5 are

D. 1 There is   2 There are

3 There are   4 There is

5 There is

[Step 1]

2 There is   3 There are

4 There is   5 There are

6 There is   7 There are

8 There are   9 There is

10 There are

[Step 2]

2 There is   a clock

3 There are   sandwiches

4 There is   some water

5 There are   pencils

6 There is   some milk

7 There are   students

8 There are   roses

9 There is   a tiger

10 There are   eggs

[Step 3]

2 There is a clock   on the wall .

3 There are sandwiches   on the table .

4 There is some water   in the cup .

5 There are pencils   on the desk .

6 There is some milk   in the glass .

7 There are students   at the playground .

8 There are roses   in the garden .

9 There is a tiger   in the zoo .

10 There are eggs   in the basket .

Unit 4. Lesson 1

Quiz Time

A.

English	Korean	English	Korean
clock/clocks	(벽에 거는) 시계	rose/roses	장미꽃
egg/eggs	달걀, 계란	sandwich/sandwiches	샌드위치
glass/glasses	유리잔	student/students	학생
pencil/pencils	연필	tiger/tigers	호랑이
playground/playgrounds	운동장	wall/walls	벽

B. 1 a/an   2 s   3 es

C. 1 buses   2 water

3 an egg   4 animals

D. 1 There is a doll

2 There are bananas

3 There is some water

4 There are (many) books

Unit 4
Lesson 2   There be 부정문

Writing에 필요한 문법 확인

A. 1 in   2 on   3 under

4 behind   5 in

B. 1 between   2 behind

3 next to   4 in front of

5 near

C. 1 There v any juice in the bottle.

2 There are ∨ any flowers in the garden.

3 There are ∨ any cars on the street.

4 There ∨ any chairs in the room.

5 There ∨ any salt in the kitchen.

D. 1 There aren't any balls on the ground.

2 There aren't any snacks in the kitchen.

3 There isn't any water in the bottle.

4 There aren't any trees behind the house.

5 There aren't any flowers in the vase.

[Step 1]

2 There aren't   3 There aren't

4 There isn't   5 There aren't

6 There aren't   7 There isn't

8 There aren't   9 There isn't

10 There aren't

[Step 2]

2 There aren't any balls

3 There aren't any cars

4 There isn't any water

5 There aren't any rivers

6 There aren't any trees

7 There isn't any milk

8 There aren't any hats

9 There isn't any soup

10 There aren't any skirts

[Step 3]

2 There aren't any balls in the box .

3 There aren't any cars in front of my house .

4 There isn't any water in the refrigerator .

5 There aren't any rivers near my town .

6 There aren't any trees next to the school .

7 There isn't any milk in the glass .

8 There aren't any hats in the store .

9 There isn't any soup in the bowl .

10 There aren't any skirts in the closet .

Unit 4. Lesson 2

Quiz Time

A.

English	Korean	English	Korean
ball/balls	공	river/rivers	강
bowl/bowls	그릇	skirt/skirts	치마
closet/closets	옷장	soup	수프
hat/hats	모자	store/stores	상점
refrigerator/refrigerators	냉장고	town/towns	마을

B.

전치사	의미	전치사	의미
in	~안에	near	~근처에
on	~위에	next to	~옆에
under	~아래에	in front of	~앞에
behind	~뒤에	between A and B	A와 B 사이에

C. 1 There aren't any trees

2 There aren't any toys

3 There aren't any pictures

4 There isn't any water

 Lesson 3 There be 의문문

Writing에 필요한 문법 확인

A. 1 A: (Yes, there is. / No, it isn't.)
2 A: (Yes, there is. / Yes, there are.)
3 A: (Yes, it is. / No, there isn't.)
4 A: (No, there aren't. / No, there isn't.)
5 A: (Yes, there is. / No, there aren't.)

B. 1 Are, No   2 Is, Yes
3 there is   4 there aren't
5 there isn't

C. 1 Is there a bicycle on the street?
2 Are there snacks in the kitchen?
3 Is there a house next to the school?
4 Are there cars behind the tree?

D. 1 Is there a book under the table?
2 Are there stars in the sky?
3 Is there juice in the glass?
4 Are there any girls on the grass?

[Step 1]
2 Is there   3 Are there
4 Is there   5 Is there
6 Are there   7 Is there
8 Are there   9 Is there
10 Are there

[Step 2]
2 Is there   juice
3 Are there   books
4 Is there   a baby
5 Is there   a bank
6 Are there   letters
7 Is there   a man
8 Are there   stars
9 Is there   a post office
10 Are there   singers

[Step 3]
2 Is there juice in the bottle ?
3 Are there books on the shelf ?
4 Is there a baby on the bed ?
5 Is there a bank near your house ?
6 Are there letters in the mailbox ?
7 Is there a man next to the tree ?
8 Are there stars in the sky ?
9 Is there a post office behind the restaurant ?
10 Are there singers on stage ?

Unit 4. Lesson 3
Quiz Time

A.

English	Korean	English	Korean
bank/ banks	은행	on stage	무대 위에
bottle/ bottles	병	post office/ post offices	우체국
letter/ letters	편지	shelf/ shelves	책꽂이, 선반
mailbox/ mailboxes	우편함	singer/ singers	가수
man/men	남자	star/stars	별

B. 1 there is   2 there isn't

   3 there are   4 there aren't

C. 1 there is   2 there aren't

D. 1 Is there coffee

   2 Are there kids

   3 Are there cookies

   4 Is there a pencil

Unit 4. Check Up

A. 1 an   2 clocks   3 is   4 foxes

B. 1 under   2 near   3 behind

   4 next to

C. 1 there are   2 there isn't

   3 there is   4 there aren't

D. 1 There are students in the
   classroom.

   2 There aren't any dogs in the
   house.

   3 Are there any benches in the
   park?

   4 There aren't any dancers on
   stage.

E. 1 There is a picture on the table.

   2 There aren't any jackets in the
   closet.

   3 Is there water in the glass?

   4 Are there cars in front of the
   house?